HOW TO THRIVE IN LA WHILE HUSTLING IN HOLLYWOOD

A how-to survive guide for creatives

Melissa Caddell

To my three delightful daughters:
Cameron, Maddy and Reece

What.a.wild.ride.

Thank you for this incredible education and to see the world through your hopes and dreams. I wrote this for you and all the creatives who see LA with deep affection and incredible possibilities.

I love you!

Cheering you on. Always. xoxo

CONTENTS

Who This Book Is For

What if I told you there was a way for you to make it as a professional creative in Hollywood, happily, and with your mental health intact? If I told you there were no secrets to being successful in the entertainment industry as an actor, writer, producer or director–that people just as new to town as you were able to hit their stride professionally, and land the job/role/project of their dreams?

People arrive in Los Angeles every day from all over the world. Do you wonder what separates the talented, hardworking creatives who grow bitter and resentful and head home after two years, from those who stay and make a successful life and career in Los Angeles? At the end of this book, you'll know how to be a successful Hollywood creative...and you'll know if you're up for it!

This book is for creatives who are willing to work hard and want some insider info on what it takes to succeed in Hollywood happily and healthily.

This book is for you if you want to pursue–or are already pursuing–a creative life as an actor, writer, creator, dancer, producer, stylist, etc. in Hollywood and are:

1) Talented enough to be here.

You are, so don't let this statement create a wave of anxiety. Somewhere along the way, someone told you that you were talented. Or more importantly, you know you are. Maybe no one has recognized it in you yet, and you came to LA because the place you were before was never going to be a place you could be the artist you want to be. The answer is yes, you are talented enough to be here. And you are just getting started, because of the next statement...

2) Growing in your craft.

This is why I don't want you to get hung up on how talented you are/think you are. To be a world-class artist in a place like Hollywood, you cannot sit on the laurels that brought you here. In fact, look at any awards, accolades or recognition you have, give them a hug of gratitude for getting you this far, and then look them firmly in the eye and declare, "This is the worst I will ever be." Get into (and stay in) classes, workshops, industry events. Get REALLY GOOD at what you do and keep going.

3) Hard working.

The professionals in this town work hard. Don't let the carefully curated social media feeds fool you. Those pretty shots were captured in between (or sometimes during) long days, long weeks, months and years. The entertainment industry is getting better, but it is not yet a very humane place for the humans involved -

insane hours, short notice, and both inflexible and constantly changing schedules are a guarantee. If that will make your life unbearable, I encourage you to educate yourself on what work you would like to do that has more regular hours and get clear on how to pursue that. Those jobs do exist and are usually the reward for years and years of hard work and proving yourself. Or they are the result of someone being very specific about how they build their career. Either way, building your reputation as someone who is responsible, trustworthy and dependable is key.

4) Have endurance.

This is THE key. This is what separates the creatives who make it in Hollywood from the ones who never achieve the goal of being a working professional here: pure stick-to-it-ness. If you are talented and growing in your craft, hardworking and have a reputation for being dependable, then this is THE THING that makes the difference between becoming a working creative professional in Hollywood and...not.

This is the secret: staying power.

In this short, powerful book, I'm going to lay out exactly what you need to do to be able to stay in LA long enough to make it. And honestly? I think you'll love it.

Note: Though I will be using language aimed at actors/writers/producers, this book is useful for anyone who is pursuing a creative career in Hollywood. There are a wide range of jobs in the entertainment industry that are artistic and innovative, and my hope is that you will know that whatever your particular area of art is, it is well-included under the term 'creatives'.

Another note: This book is NOT for you if you secretly (or not so secretly) want to be famous. Famous for what? Murder? Scandal? A funny TikTok? If your goal is to be famous for something, I would recommend you clarify what you want to be famous for and go from there.

Ok, ready? Let's go.

Why I Wrote This Book

For the past 15 years, I have stood on many darkened sets on Hollywood studio lots, asking writers, directors, actors, producers, PAs, gaffers, wardrobe stylists, makeup artists, stunt coordinators and a hundred other cast and crew designations in-between:

"What brought you to LA?"

I've also heard questions about how to 'make it' be asked and answered at enumerable casting director workshops, industry panels and conversations with agents and managers. As I watched and learned and asked questions myself, I grew in clarity around what makes Hollywood so appealing and, also, what makes it so seemingly difficult to break into: what is the difference between those who 'make it' and those who don't?

It's been an eye-opening experience. And, it turns out, people will just tell you the 'secret' to making it in Hollywood if you ask them.

I came to Hollywood with my eyes as big as saucers and alternately elated and terrified of the potential this town offered my three kids. We were not a show biz family and found ourselves moving to LA due to a series of lucky breaks that felt impossible to ignore. We didn't know anyone in the industry when we first came to visit, except an agent and manager who had scouted our eldest daughter (then age 7) from a showcase in our home state of Colorado.

My first time on a Hollywood set, I clutched my coffee from crafty as I stood to the side, kept a sharp eye on my excited small actor, and began to have conversations with the people around me: Where are you from? How long have you been in LA? How did you get started doing what you're doing?

Between three kids and hundreds of sets over 15 years (and counting), I found the people and conversations fascinating. And I learned that the stories of successful creative professionals had very similar threads.

Then I noticed I was passing along this consolidated information to more and more creatives in LA— encouraging the new PA on the set of a tv show, chatting with the writer who was my cashier at Trader Joe's, and a stream of young adult creatives who flowed through our home and community in the years my 'child' actors were stepping out into their professional lives on their own. (Warning to you if you are ever my Lyft driver—be prepared to answer these questions.)

At some point, I recognized that I was sharing the same basic principles over and over again and that they hadn't changed from the first day I accidentally kicked a light stand on that first set.

I love creatives. I am passionate about supporting you and the bravery of every creative who has chased their vision to be a working professional all the way to Hollywood. I believe that the shared stories made here, and all the people involved in creating them are a huge part of making the world a better, more loving, humane place. So, I am doing my part to take care of you—a creative human who has made a series of choices that has led you to hustling your butt off in Hollywood for the chance to be part of creating these stories.

Yes, it is hard work to break in. Would you really want it to be easy? Do you really want a low bar for entry to a place that powerfully impacts the world as much as Hollywood?

And yes, it can take time and networking—which is as it should be. Creating art in the entertainment capital of the WORLD should take as long as needed to test the mettle and conviction of the artist. Hollywood is the world's biggest billboard. Those with creative influence are in a position to impact an awful lot in the hearts and minds of the people who consume the content the world over. So, yeah, it's important to have creatives who will wield that wisely.

I may have just set Hollywood up as a daunting place of hard work and high expectations, but it IS possible to come to LA to grow your career as an actor, a writer, or in a hundred other creative arts. The thousands of hours of conversations I have had from one end of town to the other have convinced me that the most important trait you need to make it in Hollywood is endurance. (Spoiler alert—that's pretty much the secret.) But how can you stick around long enough to make it? How do you outlast the daily things that will try to wear you down and will account for the vast majority of creatives leaving LA within just a year or two of moving here?

I wrote this book for you—to give you hope and guidance on exactly what you need to discover about Hollywood and yourself to build a life you love in Los Angeleshile you wait for the phone to ring.

Note: there are a few questions for you to reflect on at the end of the chapters. While reading this book is helpful for your mindset, nothing will change in your life if you do not take some steps of action and apply what resonates with you. A special note that these are probably best answered in a cool-looking journal while you sip something tasty at a trendy cafe, looking contemplatively off into the distance.

Other note: This info holds up for New York, Atlanta, Vancouver--anywhere you specifically are to pursue your creative dream.

Chapter One - The 4 Things You Need To Know To Be A Working Professional In Hollywood

You may have noticed that there are a million talented people in Hollywood. And they are all good looking/quirky/interesting/qualified. Do not let this discourage you.

Let's assume you are talented enough to be here and are putting in the effort to get better at your craft. If these things are true, then the only thing you have to do now is outlast everyone else. You heard me right. Even taking into consideration the who-you-know factor, that's the only thing that really separates the people who 'make it' in Hollywood from those who don't.

They outlast people.
That's it.

Sure, a few lucky breaks when opportunity meets your readiness don't hurt, but if you are:

1) Talented, and

2) Growing in your craft, and

3) Hard working, then

4) You just have to stay around long enough to get known by casting directors, directors, producers and other decision makers in the industry.

And the only way to stick around long enough for the magic to happen is for you to have a life in LA that is good—one where you have friends, pursuits that restore you, and a job that supports your ability to grow in your craft and relieves financial pressure.

You have to have a life you love.

Building a life you love in LA to sustain you and help your creative soul thrive takes some time and a lot of intention. I'm going to show you how to do that so you don't quit and leave LA as a bitter and angry person. Or worse, STAY in LA as a bitter and angry person.

Industry professionals will tell you that it takes 5 -7 years to get known in this town. Known for being the person who shows up on time, ready to work, and a team player with no drama. Known for making casting (or the producer, the head writer, or the department head) look good and solving their problems.

Every year, droves upon droves of actors and creatives show up in Los Angeles with dreams and determination. Within two years, the vast majority head back home. Imagine that kind of turnover in other industries. With so many people moving in and out of Los Angeles each year, you can bet the decision-making professionals take notice of the folks who stick around and keep getting better.

Note: not everyone who comes to LA as an actor REALLY has a dream to be an actor, though they may not know it. Sometimes people just want to do something in the film and tv industry, but they don't know what other kinds of creative work is out there. The more you live here, the more you start to know what some of those roles are as you read the credits on movies or tv shows. Being an actor is the most visible job in Hollywood, so when you feel the pull to be involved in the entertainment industry, that's sometimes all you can think of.

But when you get here, your world opens up more and perhaps you get really fascinated by another aspect of storytelling you didn't even know existed. Like stunts. Or music scoring. Or costume design. Suddenly, you see where your passion for storytelling aligns with your interests and talents and voilà! you've found your niche AND your dream. If acting is what brought you here and you found a new dream as you learned more about how things work, then good for you! Or if you know you probably don't really want to be an actor and aren't sure what would make you happy, keep exploring. Being an 'actor' can be the gateway substance for the real deal for you and kudos for seeing what would make you happy and pivoting to it!

This is why building a life you love in Los Angeles as you create your Hollywood dream is so important: to stay long enough to find some of these things out about yourself and if you really DO want to make it in Hollywood.

People don't leave LA because they are happy and thriving. They leave (and often give up on their creative dreams) because they feel lost, lonely and sad.

But imagine if you knew how to stick it out long enough to get known in this town and discover what you love. Imagine when your agent submits you for a project, the casting directors are excited to bring you in and see what you'll do with the character. Imagine getting to work with cast members and crew you have crossed paths with on other sets and knowing that your reputation in the industry is solid. That people can depend on you to be professional and to be really good at what you do. That you know what you bring and are confident in how your piece fits into the whole picture of making something in Hollywood.

For all that to happen, you have to be the best version of yourself you can be. With endurance. It's all well and good to show up to your first audition off-book, bright-eyed and bushy-tailed, but can you do it for your 100th audition? It can take up to 150 auditions before you book a role. Can you continue to show up in your creative field of choice with enthusiasm for the opportunity in front of you? It's a heck of a lot easier to remain professional and optimistic if you aren't bitter and angry and don't hate your entire life in LA.

Read on for how to build a life you love in LA while you hustle in Hollywood.

Chapter One: Questions For Reflection

1) Why did you move to LA? (Or why do you want to?)

2) Have you thought about committing to living in LA for the next 5 years? What would you want it to look like in terms of a survival job, housing, friends/community?

3) Does the idea of living here for 5-7 years make you excited? Exhausted? Why do you think that is? Is that how you want it to be?

Chapter Two - Practical Tips To Build A Life You Love

The absolute best place to start in building a life you love in LA is to really know yourself and be honest about what you want and need. We can spend a lot of time and energy trying to look good or doing what other people think we should, but that will absolutely kill your chances to have a happy and healthy life. (Read that last sentence again.) Experience will tell you that a happy and healthy creative life is one where you are not overdrawn or living on the edge all the time: financially, emotionally, physically and spiritually. It impacts your capacity to handle daily life in LA as a healthy human and have the bandwidth to also be a healthy creative. Here's how:

Financially

The problem with being on the financial edge all the time is that you are mentally distracted, distressed and exude desperation - whether you mean to or not. And it is when you REALLY NEED to book that role/project/gig that you will inadvertently be really unhireable because no one wants to hire someone with the weird energy that comes from being desperate and fearful.

Financial stress also makes you more stressed about

EVERYTHING.

Give yourself as much financial margin as you possibly can. If you are one unexpected car repair away from major financial distress, your creativity will be pretty shut down. Survival mode diverts all energy and possibility thinking away from the parts of your brain that are creative.

To be healthy financially:

1. Know what amount of income you need to cover the basics of your life.
Write it down. Not knowing exactly how much you need to bring in and how much you are actually bringing in is not making it any better. Know what you need and then you'll know if you want to decrease expenses or increase income to bridge any gaps.

2. Get 3-6 months' worth of those expenses in savings.
Do NOT pass go until you do this. Trust me. When your car is towed because you didn't comprehend the 15 point parking sign and it's confusing dos and don'ts and then you can't pay rent/ for acting class/to go out after work and network, it will suck - and make you bitter and angry and hate LA. Which will wear you down and add a little weight to the column of packing up and heading back home.

3. Be careful about spending choices that are mostly (or all) about how you look to other people.
Looking successful is not the same thing as

being confident, good at what you do, and marketable. Unless your goal is to be a professional influencer. In that case, figure out how to budget that in/understand how it is a business expense/get paid to do it.

4. Know what you need to have joy in your life and budget it in.

If you need a latte every morning, don't feel guilty and shame yourself about it—budget it in and cut costs somewhere else. If you know that to be mentally healthy you must visit the ocean or an art museum or a comedy club every week, plan for it.

5. Get good at saying, 'That's not a financial priority for me right now.'

You know what IS a financial priority? The financial margin that buys you some mental health to increase your capacity to be a creative person living happily in LA. Also get good at finding alternatives to spending money to do things you enjoy. Like having someone over for coffee instead of going out, cooking food at home and picnicking instead of restaurants. Explore resources like free museum days, etc. There are a lot of those kinds of things in LA.

Emotionally

Creative people use a lot of their emotional energy just BEING in the world. And there are so.many.things that impact you. Your receptors are always on, taking in a lot of emotional information and processing it all the time. It will help you immensely to discover ways to limit the input so you do not burn out in the long run (and short run).

From a daily perspective, just getting ready to leave your apartment might use up a bunch of energy. Think of all the decisions you make to go out into the world:

- What do I wear? Which is really, 'How do I want to be perceived?'
- How do I feel about the person/event I am leaving home for?
- Is it for work? Work I like?
- Is it a place I'll need to make a bunch of small decisions, like the grocery store?
- Networking, where I might feel judged? A connection? A needy, drama-filled 'friend'?
- Something that will renew me?

When you are drained emotionally, everything feels hard. Recognize that being mindful of emotional care is an important part of being a healthy and thriving creative.

Here are some tips for emotional health:

1. Know what drains your energy and limit those things as much as possible.
If you mentally think 'ugh' when you see a text from a certain person, consider limiting your need to interact with them. If your messy apartment is emotionally stressful, make it a priority to figure out how to live well in it. Not sure what is draining you? Consider the things in your life you are complaining about or avoiding. Start there.

2. Know what fills you up emotionally and add more

of that into your daily life.

When was the last time you did something you loved? Read a book? Sipped the perfect cup of tea unhurriedly as you watched the sunset? Listened to your favorite playlist? Worked out? Ate something really really delicious? Window-shopped or looked at beautiful things? Called the person who makes you laugh?

There are so many opportunities to stop and notice and refresh. LA has some really beautiful places (I mean, have you seen Instagram? #LA). As a creative person, this is a habit that is necessary for your continued work in this world. If you are tired or overdrawn emotionally, you will struggle to have the energy you need to pour into your craft. And you certainly won't have the resources that are needed to grow as an artist. Or to be a happy human.

Do what you need to build a life where you have an abundance of emotional energy to create and to love your life.

Physically

For many creatives, their body is their instrument. This is true for actors, musicians, singers, writers, performers, lighting designers, carpenters—anyone who uses their mind or body for their work.

So...everyone here.

Your physical health impacts your ability to do your creative work. Treat yourself accordingly.

1. Eat well.

Pay attention to what you put into your body. Your body must process whatever goes into it, so be mindful about what you are giving it to deal with. Give it healthy amounts of what it needs. If you don't know what food makes you feel good physically, spend some time learning more about yourself and what you need/don't need. If this is an area of struggle for you (either under or over-eating) please find a safe place to treat yourself kindly as you grow to respect food in a healthy way. You must create a healthy relationship with it because the entertainment industry does NOT have a healthy relationship with it and will NOT be much help here. Your physical health is usually a symptom of your mental health—if you have a good relationship with your body mentally, it will come off in how you respect and treat yourself physically. This is important.

2. Sleep well.

Not only does your body need the chance to heal and repair from the daily stress of LA living, but your mind also needs the chance to rest and repair. Because your body is your instrument, it is not selfish or lame to get healing levels of sleep and rest. It is paramount to your ability to have emotional resources to deal with your life and to honor the effort you make physically every day to walk through this world. And this level of care is acknowledged. When someone says they need to leave a party/event/social gathering because they have an early call time, it is deeply respected. At least by the professionals who are making a living at their craft in Hollywood. You cannot control lots of things around schedules in LA, so be mindful around guarding your rest.

3. Move your body.

Find exercise you like to do and be consistent with your efforts to stay physically strong and healthy. I know that everyone in LA looks fit, but the vast majority of people do not have a healthy relationship with their physical bodies and I suspect a lot of people are malnourished (or undernourished) and physically weak. If you are physically weak, you will not have the strength and general endurance a creative life needs. Make friends with your body and pay attention to what feels good, makes you feel strong and moves you toward a long, healthy life. Binge cleanses aren't it. Excessive workouts aren't it. Working out healthily in a way that makes you feel happy and connected to all the awesome things your body can do, is.

Spiritually

Creatives tend to be more in tune with the spiritual anchors of awe and wonder than the general population. Whether that higher power is labeled God, Nature, the Universe, Energy, etc, creatives are often spiritually aware of forces outside themselves in this world. Because of this sensitivity, some kind of spiritual practice is a component of building a healthy life.

1. Whatever it means to you to be mindful, do more of that.

If you like to journal, make a daily habit to do so (I highly recommend *The Artist's Way* by Julia Cameron for some guided journaling). Maybe you find peace in a gratitude journal, or you practice meditation or prayer. Being aware of what you are thinking and how you are engaging with the wisdom available outside yourself is a critical way to stay balanced and grounded.

2. Connect with a spiritual community.

Lots of people in LA self-describe as spiritual, but unless there is some accountability and support for continued growth by being with like-minded humans, your spirituality can become self-focused and limited to your own understanding. Which is the opposite of the benefits of connecting with a spiritual practice and the wisdom and perspective of healthy humans. Find a safe place to question and grow this part of yourself. It's important for mental health and creative life.

If you have never had a spiritual practice and don't necessarily consider yourself a spiritual person, you may connect with this concept better as soul work. Or what is at the core of who you are. Keep yourself open to paying attention to the places and practices in your life that help you feel peaceful and connected to the world outside yourself. An artist who understands their own soul is in a better place to love and impact other humans at their core, too.

Chapter Two: Questions For Reflection

1) What is the ONE thing you could do in the next week that would decrease your financial stress?

2) What is the ONE thing you could do today that would improve your physical health?

3) What is the ONE thing you could do today that would help your mental health?

4) Do you have a healthy, like-minded spiritual community you connect with regularly?

Chapter Three - How To Create Your Ideal Physical Environment

Where you lay your head at night is going to have a profound impact on your mental health over the long term. Sure, you can crash on someone's couch/sublet in the scary part of town for the short-term, but if you are in LA to stay (at least until your career takes off in the next 5-7 years), you are going to want to put down some roots. It may take some time to discover exactly what works for you, and there are a few things to consider.

Where to live

Your home life can make or break you. It takes time, energy and resources to build your career, and unnecessary energy expenditures for daily living can slowly eat away at your reserves.

This part of your LA life needs to be built with thought and clear intentions. Know yourself, what you really want, what you are willing to compromise on, and what you know you really require in your life to maintain your creative energy and mental health.

What do you really want and need for home life? Get clear on this.

What is your idealized version of what you want your life to look like in this season? Have you always imagined pedaling your bicycle near the beach after work? Being close to the action of downtown? Or tucked away in a quiet tree-lined neighborhood? There are a lot of neighborhoods in the LA-area with a range of price-points and amenities. Know if you will have a happier life if you have designated parking when you come home from your restaurant job at 2am. Or if you are willing to fight for street parking for the benefit of an on-site gym. Or a place that allows your cat.

Whatever it is, know what you really need. When you make too many concessions in this area, it is just a matter of time before you become fixated about your annoying roommate, irate at the loud city noises through the paper-thin walls, or tired of how far everything is to drive to. All of which are unnecessary drains on your time and energy. You CAN find a good housing situation. It is worth the time and effort to do so early on in your LA life.

Really think about what you need. Will city noises like traffic, sirens and construction drain you or enliven you? If you can't get to a park or walk in nature every day, how does that impact your mental health? You are creating a life that allows you to thrive, so don't start caving on things from the get-go. Sure, you may have to make some concessions, but be really mindful about what you really cannot negotiate on to have energy and good mental health. The goal is to be happy in your actual, present life.

Roommate life

If I had a nickel for every roommate horror story I've heard in Los Angeles, I'd be able to cover the towing fee the next time I accidentally park on La Brea after 4pm.

Ideally, you have a great roommate who can help with a late-night self-tape, knows how to clean a bathroom and has a steady job. The reality is that a town like LA attracts a certain kind of person. They are either really driven, really talented, and/or really a mess.

Usually, some combination of all three. And if you're here, you are also probably some combination of that. Try not to be the super weird roommate. Or to have the super weird roommate. Trust your instincts when you are scoping someone out as a possible roommate.

If you can NOT need a roommate, consider that as an option for your mental health. Really think about what a roommate brings to the table for you. If it's just a financial decision, budget it out and see what's possible. Some people do better living with another human, but some people don't.

If you do need or want a roommate, here are some tips for how to game the roommate system:

1) Know them in real life before you live with them.
While this doesn't eliminate discovering every person's possible dysfunctional weirdness, it helps identify some of it. If you've met someone in acting class or yoga class or at work and can imagine

being pretty happily trapped with them for months and months during a global pandemic (you know, theoretically), then they may be a good candidate. I would caution against living with a boyfriend/ girlfriend. If you ever need some space from each other or things fall apart, it sucks to have to endure the stress of moving with the compound of heartbreak.

2) Get referrals.

If you don't have a relationship with a potential roommate first, I highly recommend only considering roomies via referrals from people you like and trust with life choices. If YOU don't know the person and no one you know has any connection with them, it's a dicey game of chance. Other people's perspectives are extremely valuable in decisions like this, so tap into the collective wisdom of your network.

3) Check their references and (of course) stalk their social media.

Ask questions of their references. It is not rude or unexpected to do so. It's taking care of yourself. Some questions to consider asking are:
- Their level of hygiene and tidiness in both personal and shared spaces.
- Did they participate in household chores?
- Pay rent and other expenses on time?

Ask what they liked about living with this person and what bugged them. Everyone has different needs, so what drives one person nuts might not make you stressed. It doesn't make anyone a bad person. It just makes them a good or bad roommate candidate for you.

Do a google search on them and check their social accounts. It may also be insightful to check posts that they are tagged in on social media and look at the accounts they follow.

4) Make short rental commitments.
Until you know for sure if this person/these persons will contribute to a healthy home life for you, don't get into a long rental commitment (meaning a year or more) with them.

Yes, short term leases are more expensive. And so is spending months not having a restful home environment which distracts you from your focus of building a creative career in Hollywood and a life you love in Los Angeles.

Loving your space
Once you are in an area of town that meets your needs, have found a lovely human or two to live with (or gone solo), it's time to take stock of how things are working for you in your physical space. Are there any daily irritations robbing you of time, energy and focus that could be better spent moving you closer to the creative career you want?

Is your space functional?
Do you have what you need to sleep well, work well, rest/restore well and eat well?

Is your space inspirational?

It doesn't have to be Instagramable, but imagine only having things that are beautiful, functional, restful or inspiring in your home. How would that change how you feel when your eyes open in the morning and when your key turns in the lock in the evening? Take a little bit of time and effort to make your space a home. It could be as simple as getting an actual bed frame so you aren't sleeping on the floor. Getting books or plants or art on the walls so it feels like home. Maybe you toss the janky silverware for something you don't hate every time you pick up a spoon. You may not realize how much daily irritations are wearing on you, but they do. Find out what they are for you and resolve them.

If this isn't your natural bent, guess what: you live in the most creative city on the planet. You probably know someone who could help you with creating a space that nurtures, restores, and re-energizes you. Look for resources on apartment living or interior design. But then actually DO something. Don't just gather a bunch of information. You can even start by just taking things OUT of your space that you do not love, that do not inspire you or are not useful (including broken things and things that are worn out or gross). Then really consider what to put in your space that will add to why you love living in LA.

Chapter Three: Questions For Reflection

1) Does your housing situation provide the energy you need (peaceful, energizing, or inspiring, etc) for you to be happy and creative?

2) What are the three most significant things you know you need in your home life to be happy and healthy?

3) What is ONE thing you could do in the next week to improve your physical environment?

Chapter Four - How To Discover Your Best Survival Job

For most creatives, doing creative work for their job is actually a terrible idea.

While it seems like a natural fit at first (singing telegrams are a great way to keep my vocal skills honed!), it can be surprisingly annoying, then draining. Over time, it's possible to get a bit resentful as you realize you have no energy left to work on your own projects or other things that would move you in the direction of your creative career. It's not true for every creative, so know what kind of 'day job' makes sense for you.

You see why so many actors and writers work in bars and restaurants. It's usually decent money, flexible hours with a pool of backups if you need the day off for that commercial you just booked, and most importantly, it doesn't drain the life force from you. Unless you are more introverted and find people to be draining. In which case, look for positions that aren't customer facing.

I do feel like there are a lot of jobs beyond bars and

restaurants that might fit the bill (consider shift work in a hospital or other medical facility, teaching private lessons, or temp office work). But being a server is a classic for a reason.

Tips for your non-career work life:

1) Be honest.

For reals. I mean, employers will point blank ask you if you are an actor because they often hate hiring actors. But do you really want to work somewhere where you have to lie about your life all the time? I promise there are a thousand jobs in LA you are qualified for. Find one where you can be honest about your skills and your expectations.

2) Know what kind of work will kill your soul.

Don't do that kind of work.

3) If the job sucks or is a toxic environment or the manager is out to get you - quit.

You do not need this kind of grief in your life. And unless your goal is to make their small business a thriving company with a level of commitment NO ONE ASKED FOR, really think about if your loyalty to a job aligns with why you came to Los Angeles. Please be an excellent employee, for sure. But unless your goals have changed since you came to LA to be a professional creative, do your job well and then make sure you aren't caught up in a job that is NOT YOUR FUTURE.

If you find yourself quitting a lot/are unable to hold

down a job, really think about the jobs you are taking and if you should be taking them. Trust your instincts at the beginning of a job—if you think it's not going to work out, tap out ASAP.

4) Be dependable.

Do you know why employers will ask you point blank if you're an actor? Because flaky, dishonest actors/creatives gave the whole profession a bad name (or maybe the employer is a bitter and angry former actor who hates their life in LA). Tips:

- Don't call out when you do not absolutely have to (actual illness or work for your creative career)
- Clearly communicate with your boss
- Work hard when you are there, and
- Don't be a jerk

I know you aren't here to climb the corporate barista ladder. But you will earn yourself a lot of favor by only calling out when you really know it's important and with as much notice as possible. It will probably be less angrily received if you try to get your shift covered. Do favors for other co-workers when you can to build up some credit and thus, be in a position to be owed a favor down the road.

Chapter Four: Questions For Reflection

1) Even if you are currently working a survival job, what are 5 other types of jobs you could do that might be a good fit for income, flexibility, and being fun or at least non-draining?

2) If you had to find a new job tomorrow, what would you do? Do you have resources/knowledge/a network in place?

3) If you are currently working a survival job, are you happy there? Does it serve your financial/mental/physical/emotional health? If not, what about the job keeps you there?

Chapter Five - How To Protect And Strengthen Your Mental Health

You are the only one who will safeguard your mental health.

Lemme say that again.

You are the only one who will safeguard your mental health.

The entertainment industry has a bit of an, er, exploitive reputation, maybe you've heard? Still, sometimes it comes as a shock how inhumane the industry can be. And how individual personal health and mental health needs/boundaries are, well, largely disregarded. Things are changing, but currently, most projects are not very healthy for the humans they employ.

And it's nothing personal, it's just business. It is called show BUSINESS for a reason. And in this context, business equals money. Decisions are almost always about money.

I've been on set and watched a young actor break down crying because they were beyond tired/hungry/ frustrated. Aside from a few moments of comfort, the basic question for the hundred or so people in the cast and crew watching the event unfold was, 'How much of a delay is this going to cause us?' Not because they are monsters, but because time is, quite literally, money. Shooting schedules are generally extremely tight with very little to no wiggle room for unexpected delays. Things are timed to the exact minute.

As harsh as it sounds, you do not want to be too risky to hire. Can you imagine trying to build a professional reputation and the comments in casting or production rooms go something like, "Yeah, they're really good, but... (he's flakey, she doesn't communicate well, he always has some kind of drama going on, etc)."

Does that mean that actors who have a need for an accommodation aren't hired or hireable? Heck no–they do and they are! As long as the request for accommodation is asked for and planned for, it's not an issue. We are all humans who are impacted by things like illness, mental health, trauma and circumstances around us. It's the things production cannot anticipate and plan for that can create a negative work experience.

This is not to say that you cannot have mental or physical health needs! How can you not? You are a sensitive, empathetic human who taps into the range of human emotions to do your job! You also require a lot out of your physical body to do the work asked of you.

What it means is that YOU are in charge of taking care of yourself so that you are fully able to do the work at hand. And advocating for yourself in a professional manner and with advance notice, when at all possible.

So if something happens unexpectedly in your world that will impact what you need to do the work you have been hired for, it is your responsibility to communicate that to your team. Maybe you know you will require your therapy dog to be in a chaotic set environment, or you have specific dietary requirements on set - make sure your manager or agent knows and have them advocate for you.

Bottom line: you don't want any 'buts' after your name is suggested. What you want is, "They're great–really professional and easy to work with."

Chapter Five: Questions For Reflection

1) Do you absolutely know what you need in your life to do your best work?

2) Are you able to advocate for yourself to your team and ask for what you need?

3) If you aren't sure about what you need or how to ask for what you need, take some time to get clear about this and how you want to communicate it. If you know and your team knows, you can be set up for success. If you or your team doesn't know, it's possible that there may be a crisis or emergency brewing. No one needs that–including you.

Chapter Six - How To Be Good (And Growing) At Your Craft So You Thrive

Remember why you moved to LA? The specific creative work that you want to be involved with? At some point in being busy trying to survive, you might have looked up and realized it had been a hot minute since you were taking steps into that industry. Maybe you've been waiting for life to be all set up before you jumped in and now that you're ready to jump, it's like you're the kid at the top of the high dive who lost their nerve a little. It seemed like such a good idea, but the longer it took you to climb the stairs and walk out on the wobbly plank to actually, you know, JUMP...well, you might have forgotten how fun it looked when you started.

But the whole reason you've made the climb to be ready to jump is because of the daring, wild adventure that awaits! It's okay if it's a little scary. Everyone here is scared at some point. What makes it significantly less scary is to be good at your craft. To be ready to dive in and make it as a professional creative in LA, you want to be really, really, really good at what you do.

You are surrounded by master craftspeople in Hollywood. Not only did these folks have the guts to move here and the endurance to stay, but as working professionals, they are rubbing elbows with the best of the best in the world at what they do. So if you wanna hang at that level, you have to keep growing in your craft.

As part of my initial conversation when I coach people who are creatives, I ask: What's your dream role? Or what kind of show/film/project would be your dream? (Sometimes people have a hard time articulating this, so it's definitely worth your time to get really clear about it.) And once they are clear on the kind of job they would pinch themselves to have, I ask them if they're ready for it.

For example, if you're an actor and a casting director called you to ask about specific skills which might be required for that dream role—are you good to go?

If your dream role is to be on a period drama and you don't know how to ride a horse or do various British accents, would you be ready for your dream role if you had a shot at it? Or if you want to be in a Sci-Fi movie and you don't have at least a basic knowledge of scientific terminology, weapons training or familiarity with stunts, well.... I have some questions for you about what you really want. And it's okay if that's NOT what you really want, but thinking you want something and then not doing the work to be ready for the chance when it comes your way is a surefire way to end up depressed and bitter.

Want to be a comedy writer? When was the last time you went to a comedy show? Musician? Do you know the music stores/classes/part of town working musicians frequent? When's the last time you took a class/practiced a skill/got GOOD at something?

Do you see what I mean? Getting good at specific skills not only keeps you moving forward, it also keeps you on people's radars. You better believe that if a project needs actors with chef skills or actors with martial arts training, the places in Hollywood that offer those classes will likely get a call from a casting director with the question of: 'Hey, are any of your students actors?'

Happens all the time. Be ready when those opportunities come.

Grow in your craft

The onus is on you to grow in your craft. The one you want to be known for. When I hear that a client has stopped going to classes/stopped taking lessons, I am instantly curious about why. If it's financial, we figure out how to solve that problem. If it's feeling worn out, we look at where they might need some intentional rest and where to add joy and delight into their lives.

When the only things you need to make it as a professional creative in Hollywood are to be dependable, stick around long enough for people to know who you are, and be GOOD AT WHAT YOU DO...growing in your craft is the action step you can take every day to be ready when you get the opportunities you moved here for.

Which may bring you to this problem: There are a lot

of classes in Los Angeles. How do you know which ones/ which people are great for skill-building, mental health and creating a sense of thriving?

Some tips on how to find resources and select classes

1) If you have an agent or manager, ask them where they recommend that their clients go. They will usually have clients with recent experiences at places all over town and they know which of their clients are growing as professionals. (And probably booking work.)

2) If you don't have an agent or manager, call the offices you would like to have as your agent or manager and ask whoever answers the phone: What acting class/writing class/voice class do you recommend for your clients? Is cold-calling like this gonna work? Maybe! Maybe they don't clarify if YOU are their client (note the wording in the question). If they do ask if you are a client, you can say: 'Not yet!'

3) Once you get into a community of working creatives (in your dance class, your aerial arts class, your screenwriting class, etc) ask the teachers and students there for referrals to other programs and classes. The places you hear about from multiple sources are good ones to try out. Most of the reputable places I know about have a free trial class (or a low-cost trial class). Trust your instincts, keep looking until you find a place you can grow for a while, and try new studios/lessons/teachers. If you've been at the same place for more than a year or so and you aren't

booking work/getting better auditions, etc, what you might have is a nice community (very important), but it may be time to also find a place where you aren't so comfy so you can stretch and grow.

A note if you are in a situation where you cannot afford to take classes in your field: in the long term, you gotta figure this out. Unless your goal was to move to LA and NOT make it, the only way you will get better is to get around other people who are better than you and keep stretching as a creative.

In the short-term, take all the free intro classes you can. Watch movies and study them. Go down the list of Oscar winners from the past 20 years and examine the performances, the writing, the directing. Watch interviews with actors, writers, directors. Read, read, read. (If you do not already have an LA County library card, go get one post haste and utilize every resource they have to access books, trade magazines, ebooks, and watch movies for free.)

There is literally zero excuse to not be growing in your craft. So if you aren't, that's something to get curious around and figure out why you don't want to.

Chapter Six: Questions For Reflection

1) How are you growing in your craft right now?

2) Do you know what your dream job is? What skills do you want to get good at to be ready for it?

3) What possible barriers do you see to leveling up your skill level? Finances? Knowing what to do next? Confidence to step up to the next level? Consider how this may be stopping you.

Chapter Seven - How To Get, Keep And Fire An Agent Or Manager In Hollywood

The three most important things you need to know about hiring an agent or manager is this:

1. You do NOT pay an agent or manager to find you work.

2. You do NOT pay an agent or manager to find you work.

3. You do NOT pay an agent or manager to find you work.

They work off a set commission when you book work. Therefore, there is no incentive on their part to bring someone into their agency who they do not think has the capacity (now or in the future) to make them money. This should give you some hope that when you DO sign with an agent or a manager, they believe you are capable of booking work in Hollywood or have the potential to.

That being said, how you feel about your agent or manager (your representation or your team) can strongly impact your sense of thriving in LA. Your team can also dramatically impact your professional career, so it is important to find a team that you feel is rooting for you, is STILL rooting for you, and if they are NOT rooting for you, how to fire them without burning any bridges. It's a small town.

How to get an agent or manager in Hollywood

There are a million stories about how people find agents and managers. And while I know you came here and hoped an agent would stop you while you were strolling casually down the street looking particularly adorable, that is such a rare event that even I, an eternal optimist, scoff at the thought now that I know how Hollywood works.

A couple of things I've heard over the years from unsuccessful actors, "You don't need an agent or manager," "They just take your money." Please note that I have only ever heard this from actors who are NOT working at a professional level. There is the rare story of someone who booked something on their own that was career making, but unless you have something really unique about you, not having an agent or manager will ultimately hurt your professional career.

Yes, you can self-submit for roles on projects without an agent or manager. And you absolutely should be doing that unless your team tells you not to. Getting onto those self-submitted projects is a great way to start building your reputation, learn about how things work in LA, and get experience. But overall, self-submission is for the beginning stages of your career. It is not for career growth.

Here's what you need to know about how to find an agent and manager:

1) Go where they are.

This generally does not mean their office (ESPECIALLY if you aren't invited!). The best advice I can give you on this is to take acting classes where they have some sort of showcase or industry events for their students. In fact, I would really consider avoiding any acting studio that does not offer this (at least for their more advanced courses). A well-connected acting studio will invite their friends and colleagues (agents, managers, casting directors, etc) who are scouting for new talent to a workshop or event and get to show you off. Sometimes, a very established acting coach may be willing to call a few places to pitch you. This is an incredible opportunity. Be ready to make your acting studio look good by YOU being as good and ready for this as possible.

2) Ask your network.

As you meet people (because you are in class, or connecting with like-minded creatives, or just generally enjoying your life and meeting folks in LA) it is totally appropriate to ask if their manager or agent is taking on new clients. In fact, if you know someone who loves their team and it seems their team likes to work with them, agents and managers REALLY like personal referrals. I would be cautious and not ask someone who would potentially be going out for the exact same roles as you, because that feels weird, but if someone talks about their team in a positive way, ask if they would connect you. And then be ready in the future to do the same for the person who asks you.

3) Call the agencies or management companies you want to work with and pitch yourself.

To do this, you must have professional headshots (taken in Los Angeles) that you can send. It helps if you have some credits (even from back home), video clips to send along, interesting skills, or a physical attribute that is in-demand in the industry (like hair color, ethnicity, etc). If an agent or manager is looking for something specific that you bring, it could open a door.

Note: If you are just starting out and do not have any representation, I recommend you start by finding a manager. They are usually on the lookout for new talent more often than an agency. Agents usually have a smaller group of clients on their roster than managers do. Managers are also more likely to take on someone with little to no credits if they see potential. Once you get a manager, they will help make introductions to agents they know once they feel you are ready.

Your goal is to find a team you believe to be supportive and who you feel is thrilled to have you signed as a client. Your team needs to be raving fans of yours. Do not sign up with an agency just because they are interested in you, or because they are large or a top agency. Sign with them if you feel like they are thrilled to work with you. YOU bring the money-making possibility. There is no shortage of great agencies in Hollywood. Find the people who are happy you are there.

5 ways to keep an agent or manager happy

Once you have a team that you feel is rooting for you, build a good relationship with them. This is absolutely paramount to thriving in LA. I cannot state this enough. It is really important for them to know you, to know about you and for you to stay connected to them. It is your responsibility to do so—do not expect them to reach out to you for this. It is on YOU to reach out to them.

How do you build a good relationship with your team?

1) Be an excellent communicator.

I cannot stress this enough. Calls and emails from them are your top priority. Do not miss their calls. If you do miss a call, respond ASAP. You are training them how to treat you. Imagine the difference it makes when they know you are their most dependable and communicative client. If you go out of town, they know in advance and with your dates. If you have a show/performance/exhibit coming up, you have invited them. If you have gained a skill, you update them. You DO NOT ghost them. Respond to any requests promptly and succinctly.

2) It is your job to educate your team about who you are and what you bring to the table.

Do not assume they know what is happening in your life. I'm not saying to call them everyday (please don't), but an email once a week to update them on anything that they would benefit to know is a great way to stay connected and keep them up to date. Remember the part where you are a creative commodity? The more they know about you, the more easily marketable you are. Took an art class? (skill!) Had great notes from a casting director at a workshop? Met a producer at an industry event (or at your job as a server)? Keep them up to date.

It also keeps your name present in their mind. The healthily squeaky wheel gets the grease, not the annoying, full-of-drama and problems wheel. Your goal is to make interactions with your team professional, easy and as delightful as possible. I highly recommend you ask them the best way to communicate with them about these things. Maybe they prefer a phone call every so often. Maybe they only want these updates via email.

Ask. They are on your side. Make their job easy.

3) PHYSICALLY visit your team AT LEAST 4 times a year.

I am always AMAZED at people who are lucky enough to have an agent or manager and who haven't bothered to physically be in their presence in far too long. They are trying to market you to Hollywood. It helps your team to see you and remember how awesome you are, your energy, and why they signed you. You are not a nuisance. They WANT to know you.

Call and ask when you can stop by. It helps to bring a little gift like fresh flowers, a shareable treat, or a small home-made snack or fruit basket. Keep in mind common dietary needs (like vegan or gluten-free). Do not stress about this and it is not an every-visit thing. It's just a little something that shows you thought of them.

4) Do NOT make them look bad.

This town is built on relationships—for your agent and manager, too. If you are late to auditions, aren't prepared, or generally unprofessional in any way, not only does it reflect poorly on YOU, but it also reflects poorly on your team.

No matter how cute or talented you are, if you damage your agent or manager's relationship with a casting office, you will be dropped faster than you can get a parking ticket. This does not mean you aren't allowed to ever have a bad day, an anxious moment or to miss an important detail in the email, but when those things happen, apologize, let your team know what happened ASAP, and create as little hassle as possible for the people impacted.

5) There really is no such thing as a permanent blacklist in Hollywood.

If you make a mistake, be humble, take ownership of what is yours to own and be better next time. Making mistakes is generally forgivable. Being an arrogant asshole about it is the thing that is harder to get past.

When to fire your agent or manager

Yes, people change agents and managers. And depending on the contract terms, some people do it regularly when they feel like their team isn't working hard for them, though that's hard to be certain about. So much work goes on that never amounts to something you see. A good team is pitching you and making phone calls for you every week. You never hear about the calls and emails that, for whatever reason, don't end in an audition. There are often a lot of connections and relationships being made for you that you won't ever see.

Honestly, if you have followed the steps above to "Keep your agent or manager", you'll know how things are going and if they are rooting for you.

If you feel like things aren't going well for you professionally, I highly recommend you advocate for yourself in this town. Very few people will do it for you, so if you do not believe your team is excited to root for you, get really clear on if it's true and what to do about it.

1) If you aren't booking work, get feedback as to why.

While I hate the term 'realistic', do be aware of what is a reasonable number of auditions to go on before you book anything (it's pretty close to 150, last I saw). Also, the first question your team is probably going to ask you when you call to inquire about this is: 'Are you in class?' If you aren't booking, either you aren't going out on auditions that are a good fit for you (a conversation to have with your team) or you are not yet bookable. Get curious as to why.

2) If you aren't getting auditions, find out why.

There are so many reasons for this, and some that have nothing to do with you, your talent or marketability. That is why constant communication with your team is key. Even something like a box that was mis-checked on a casting website that indicates you aren't available (true story) is easily and quickly noticed when your team is aware of what is happening in your life.

If you aren't getting auditions because your team doesn't really get you or your type, that warrants a conversation with them.

If you aren't getting auditions because they aren't pitching you for roles, then that is definitely a conversation to have with them.

How would you answer the question: how am I training my team to see me?

In the end, if you get the sense that they don't believe in you or that their needs have changed since they signed you, ask them if they are still excited to work with you. If you don't think they are, consider moving on. I say this carefully, because when in doubt, stay. And I will tell you that it is easier to get another agent or manager while you have one. If you do start looking for new representation while you are still with your current team, make it clear to your new prospective team why you are considering leaving your current team, don't blame, and ask them for discretion.

Have I mentioned that this is a small town? Word gets around about problem clients. If you feel like you really need to fire your team, know that the next agent or manager you talk to will definitely call them up to see what their perspective is.

Loyalty is important, but it must go both ways for anyone to make any money.

My team let me go: some perspective

Good, professional actors get let go by their teams and it is not a fatal event. There are a lot of reasons actors get let go that often have to do with the agent or manager or the market or something unrelated to the actor, personally. They may let clients go who are not booking, or perhaps the market need has changed and they don't need a certain type anymore. Maybe they have multiple actors of the same type (like athletic blonde men, 18-24 years old), and the more experienced actor is the one they are hanging on to. Having a good relationship with your team can protect against this to some degree, but ultimately, it's show business and if you aren't booking work, they aren't getting paid.

Maybe you could argue that you aren't booking work because you aren't getting auditions from your team. Do you know why you aren't getting auditions? Is it you? Is it the industry? You can see how really good communication will keep this from being any sort of surprise.

Ultimately though, you don't want to be with an agent or manager who is no longer excited about you. It's okay to let go of that relationship and find a new team that will be excited to work with you. Consider why you got let go, what part of it is on you, and take what you have learned about yourself and how you want to be in relationship with your team into the new relationship.

Do. Not. Burn. Bridges. You can end business partnerships without losing your professionalism. You never know when your paths may cross with them in the future.

What if you got let go for something you did wrong?

I've seen agents take on problematic clients that left another agency, so it's not like you won't ever work in this town again if you have had some self-inflicted challenges. But know that getting an offer of representation is a risk from an agent or manager under the best of circumstances. If you are not operating under the best of circumstances, be intentional about building trust. Agents and managers take on clients they hope will get hired and they do a lot of work for you before they ever earn a dime. If you've got baggage, recognize it is extra work for them to get you hired.

If you are happy and thriving in LA, you can see how the business side of life will be less devastating when things don't go the way you want them to. Endurance is as much of a skill in pursuing your craft as it is in finding the right team. The most assured way to advance in your career in Hollywood is to make raving fans of the people who meet you. Acting coaches, casting directors, agents and everyone who knows someone who knows someone. Chin up. Spirits up. Talent up. You are building relationships with everyone, all the time. Being a happy person in the midst of all of this will make building good and life-giving relationships in Hollywood about a million times more possible.

Chapter Seven: Questions For Reflection

1) If you do not have representation yet, what is your next step to find a manager/agent?

2) If you do have representation, how would you rate yourself as a client?

3) What can you do (now or in the future) to be your team's favorite client? What is in your control around this relationship?

Chapter Eight - A Law For Thriving Creatives: Do Not Wait To Be Chosen

One of the most disheartening things about being a creative is living with the idea that you are waiting to be chosen. Waiting for someone to deem you or your talent as worthy.

That thinking will rob you of all joy and will slowly make you a bitter and angry actor/writer/creative in LA.

It is also incorrect.

Sure, an agent or a casting director or a producer or some person in power may be a decision maker on a project you want to work on, but there are SO MANY creative projects that need humans to work on them and there is no shortage of work in Los Angeles for the people who are ready for it.

Here's the thing: if you are waiting to be chosen, you forget who holds the power.
You do.
Hollywood needs creatives.

You don't need Hollywood to be a working creative. You can take whatever creative thing you do and get paid to do it somewhere else. Actors and writers and set designers can work in lots of places in the world. Contact me if you think of something I haven't, but with 20 years of experience with and around tv and film, I cannot think of a single artistic pursuit that is only localized to Hollywood.

Every day, the movers and shakers in Hollywood wake up and hope for someone to solve a creative problem for them. They need a director for a project, or a kick-ass special effects team, or a solution to a scheduling problem they just cannot see their way around. They need content, content, content! Writers, actors, musicians, dancers, performers, artists - creatives of all kinds!

You embody a powerful commodity in Hollywood–the capacity to create something new. You are the magic makers. The storytellers. The world-builders.

Don't forget who holds the ultimate power in Hollywood—if you're not sure, google any union strike that has happened in LA and see what happens when creatives in the industry remember who holds the cards.

Yes, creativity is a marketable commodity. And yes, it sure is nice when someone selects you as the perfect fit for a project. But don't wait around to get chosen. As long as you are:

1) Talented, and

2) Growing in your craft, and

3) Hard working, and you

4) Stick around

You will work in Hollywood.

But if you grow angry and resentful about the waiting, lose patience with the whole system, grow arrogant, or think you need a particular role, connection, or project to hire you, you will reek of bad juju and desperation. And that is what creates a weird energy or neediness with every interaction you have in the industry. If you do not know who you are and what you bring to the table, you may come across as hyper-charming, hyper-agreeable, and hyper-needy. I've watched it happen time and again on a set with creatives who have forgotten that THESE THINGS COULD NOT EXIST without the contribution they bring, and it makes me cringe.

No one wants to work with clingy, needy, angry, arrogant, desperate people.

Know your power. Know what you bring. Be so good and easy to work with that they cannot ignore you.

With that said...

What are you responsible for in your career in Hollywood?
Just pause for a moment and consider who you would be as an artist if you weren't focused on making everyone around you happy. Consider if you knew there was an ABUNDANCE of work for talented, hardworking, endurance-full creatives in LA.

How would you show up to your next audition?

How would you approach the next thing you made to send along to someone to be 'chosen' for a project? Would you be anxious? Annoyed at minor inconveniences? See the other actors in the waiting room as competition?

I imagine if you knew your work speaks for itself and knew you would get the projects that are meant for you, it would be a lot more fun. I bet you might take some creative risks. That you would work on your own projects. And that you might see each chance to connect with other humans in the industry from a place of gratitude.

I am talking about a balance of being hungry, humble, and confident. Hungry enough to not wait around to be noticed by a decision maker, humble enough to consider each connection and opportunity respectfully, and confident that you are ready to go when an opportunity to work hard and show up as your talented self opens up in front of you.

I am not talking about an attitude of arrogance. Being arrogant will earn you a reputation for being difficult to work with and you will likely have a short run in this town. Arrogance shuts you down to possibility and you get very concerned about what is 'due' to you. That occurs to me as a terrible place to collaborate with people from.

So, what is in your control?

    1) Being good at what you do. (See chapter 5)

    2) Noticing what you think when you don't get an audition/callback/hired for a project.

Do you blame other people? Your team? Your acting coach? Your college program that didn't prepare you for this?? If you are pointing a finger at anyone other than yourself for how things are going for you in LA, then I imagine your life in Los Angeles may be pretty miserable.

And probably short.

3) You are in control of how you are training people to see you.

Want to be seen as a fantastic actor? Be a fantastic actor. A writer with mad ingenuity? Then be a writer with brave and bold ingenuity. A hilarious content creator? You get the idea. You are training your agent, your acting teacher, that casting director, even the cashier at Trader Joe's—how to see you. You are teaching people what kind of person you are and how you show up as an artist in this world.

Please do not read this as you must be happy and perfect at all times. Fake happiness is a terrible, horrible, draining burden that serves no one.

It means that how you respond to events in your career and life in LA are what BUILDS your life in LA. (See Chapter 4 for tips on how to manage some of this.)

Stop waiting for people to give you permission to create the art you want and start creating it. Wanna do a sitcom about your weird family? Start with short videos and get clear on your ideas as you actually make stuff. Want to write horror musicals? What's stopping you? Write them and then throw a rock to find other creatives in LA who will generously and gladly give up hours of their lives to play and create it with you.

There are no gatekeepers to creating things. And when you are creating things, you are happy and thriving. When you are happy and thriving and not waiting to be chosen is when you will exude a humble gratitude for where you get to live and the people in your life and it's really hard not to want to hire someone like that.

Chapter Eight: Questions For Reflection

1) What would you do, creatively, if you had 'permission' to do it? (Consider that being chosen is really just permission to use time, money and resources to create something. What if you gave it to yourself?)

2) Who or what do you notice yourself blaming (even inside your head) when your LA life is not going the way you want it to? Is it true that it is their fault?

3) How are you really training people to see you? Is that the way you want them to see you?

Chapter Nine - How To Know
When It's Time To Quit

Dear Creative - did you skip to this chapter first? It's okay. I bet you're exhausted and tired of wondering how long you can last in the often-grueling crush of LA.

May I suggest a nap and a snack? And then go back to the beginning of the book.

And then...

When should you quit trying to make it in LA?
This is a hard question. And it may be one you keep shoving into the dark corners of your mind to make it shut up. If you are using how you feel about trying to make it in LA as a measure of progress, stop. The emotional ups and downs of the entertainment industry are a terrible way to judge your progress on how you are actually doing in the industry.

Are you hanging on until something specific happens in your life or career? Do you have a plan for when you will tap out of LA? Perhaps you came to Hollywood with a solid idea that this was a time-limited event for you and if you don't 'make it' by a certain date (whatever your version of making it means), you know you'll head home. But maybe you're just gritting your teeth and holding on.

First, I want to be clear what question I am answering:

1) Are you asking if you should quit trying to be a professional creative in LA? Or,

2) Are you asking if you should quit pursuing your craft in general? Or,

3) Are you wondering if it's okay to switch your goal to something you discovered a passion for while on your journey as an actor/writer/creative in Hollywood?

Because if you came here with a very specific dream to be a professional actor in film/tv and along the way to become that you discovered a different kind of thing that you are super excited about—then heck yeah! Chase the thing that is raising your pulse! (Unless it's a person—don't chase a person.)

You do not have to justify this to anyone—it's like if you went to college to study architecture and along the way came across a subject you didn't even know was a job (like being a theme park engineer). When you fell head-over-heels for it, wouldn't you change majors and pursue designing roller coasters happily for the rest of your life? Without guilt or shame that you didn't become an architect.

If you're worried about telling the folks back home

that a) no, you haven't worked on anything they've seen, and b) you're quitting acting/writing/whatever the thing is you said you came to Los Angeles to pursue, then may I lovingly tell you to snap the hell out of it? This is YOUR one and only precious life. Live it how you want to.

If you want to be part of the entertainment industry and you have found a way to do it in a job you love as you build a life you love—wahoo! Do it!

If along the way you found something not entertainment related that you would never have known about if you hadn't discovered it while living in LA, then take it as a freaking win and a gift from the universe that has set you on a path that fills you with life and joy.

Your journey does not have to end with the destination you intended to be a really happy life for you. Do you know ANY happy people who have never pivoted? How many great stories start with, 'Well, I came here to do X, but I discovered Y, and fell in love with it.' A lot. Trust your instincts.

If we are paying attention, the journey always leads us to our sweet spot—where our talents, strengths and passions meet. Notice where you come alive, what you love, and what you choose to spend your time on.

Still reading because I haven't answered your question? Have you had that snack and nap yet? Because here it is. If you are:

1) Talented, and

2) Growing in your craft, and
3) Hard working, then
4) You just have to stay around long enough to be known by casting directors, directors, producers and other decision makers in the industry.

The only way to fail to be a professional creative in Hollywood is to quit.

And quitting is a totally acceptable choice. There is NO SHAME in deciding you've had enough and you want something different. Do you hear me on that? The price is HIGH. It can be TOO HIGH. It can take a toll on your mental health, your physical health, your financial goals and your personal dreams.

It is OKAY to say, 'Welp, this was an interesting ride! I am gonna take the things I learned and head back to Texas (or wherever) and build a different life there.'

You came, you saw, you learned a ton about yourself, the world, the ins and outs of the entertainment industry and you can choose to tap out when the ride is not aligned with your vision for your life.

What I would strongly caution against is quitting because you are tired. Quitting because it's really hard. Quitting because it seems to be taking forever. No quitting decisions should be made late at night, after getting (another) parking ticket, when you didn't get the part you really wanted (again) or when you are generally exhausted or hangry.

Absolutely move on if you have a new vision for your life. Absolutely move on if you have learned that what you thought would bring you joy ISN'T. Do NOT hang on for hanging-on's sake. GET OUT IF IT SUCKS.

But, don't leave because it's not happening for you yet. If it's not happening and you are growing weary, pivot. Try something new with your craft. Backtrack to the last time you remember having FUN as you learned and grew and figure out WHY it was fun. Add more of that into your life. Move apartments. Get a cat. Change your day job. Get new headshots. Enroll in circus school and learn how to juggle fire. DO SOMETHING that re-engages you with the things you love in your life, and what you love about LA. Maybe you need to take a trip OUT of LA so you remember why you love it.

But be clear on what you are doing and why so that you never look back and think, 'I wish I would have....'. Leave on your terms and for a new vision.

If you are miserable in LA trying to pursue your craft, that is on you. Yes, there are a LOT of freaking things that make it hard. But LA is the most creative city on the planet. There is SO much possibility here. 'What if' hums through the dangerously uneven sidewalks, in every strangely nondescript casting room and through the hands of every barista/screenwriter.

I don't know that every creative person can thrive and live their best life in LA. Talented, hardworking, endurance-full people leave and have happy lives pursuing their craft in other places in the world (sometimes in places with more affordable housing).

What I want is for you to choose to leave. Not to sneak out of town in the dead of night, ashamed of what you haven't done. Don't leave on an anti-dream—one where you just hate what your life is but you don't know what you want aside from 'not this'.

It's okay to leave when you're done. Take the lessons and your Erewhon Market tote and leave with your head held high. Man, the stories you can tell, am I right? And the wisdom and insight and experience are yours to keep and employ wherever you go next.

But if your heart aches too much at the thought of leaving, it's not time to go. It might not ever be time to go. Or maybe it will be on the other side of a well-developed career you love.

Magic happens here every day. Lives change on a phone call. Every day.

Your day is coming.

Chapter 9: Questions For Reflection

1) Have you thought about when/if you will leave LA? What keeps you here right now?

2) If you decided to leave LA tomorrow, what would you do next? How do you feel about that idea?

3) What can you do this week to reignite the fun of pursuing your craft in LA?

Chapter Ten - Your Hero's Journey

If you've taken a creative writing or screenwriting class, you might have heard the advice about writing the life of your characters: **Make it worse, make it worse, make it worse.**

We want things to be difficult for our protagonist/hero because that's how they grow.

And it's the same for all of us. Comfort does not equal growth. Don't be afraid of discomfort. Of doing hard things. You are literally MADE to bloom and grow in adversity. It is the law of nature. Have you SEEN the flowers pushing their way through the crack in the sidewalk?

Life is designed to thrive. And so is yours.

The things you are going through are shaping you as a human and as a creative and those experiences are the literal tools you will use as you keep growing as an artist. You are gaining life experience and that will make you a better artist. You can't communicate the essence of humanity through your creative endeavors if you do not experience life! Embracing the discomfort of growth and development will make you a better human, too.

Artists who have seasons of thriving are much better able to handle all the crap that LA might throw at you when it gets rough. It's not LA and it's not that you are an artist, it's that life provides never-ending opportunities for you to see what you're made of. For sure, it can feel like it's coming harder and faster in LA.

You will have bad days. And the weather won't even get un-perfect to allow you to wallow in your misery. Oh no, you're going to have to pull your blinds closed and crank your a/c up to make it seem like it's a dreary day outside to match your foul mood.

Your car will break down the same week your significant other decides they want to see other people, which will be the same time you won't get that role you really wanted, and your cat will get expensive sick and your roommate will suddenly be having an emotional meltdown and be totally unavailable to HELP YOU, FOR THE LOVE OF ALL THINGS LOS ANGELES.

And that's ok.

Because what doesn't kill you makes you stronger. Or wiser. Sometimes both.

And when those annoyingly perfect weather days keep a comin' despite the trauma and drama around you, you'll start to hit your stride as a creative person who can live happily here. Every little thing that can make your relationship with LA, erm, 'complicated', won't take you out the way it once did.

Because you will have bandwidth to absorb it. You'll have friends, support, community, emotional and financial margin. You'll have things you love, activities that refresh you and maybe a little bit of affection for the City of Angels.

It's okay if you hate LA–lots of people do. But I don't think those are the people who are thriving in their chosen profession here.

The choice is yours, of course. I've heard it said that LA is tough on people because we're all takers—only interested in what the city can do for us. So yeah, she's got some baggage around the creatives who file in year after year, looking for what Hollywood can do for them. Maybe show her some love, ya know? Show her you can commit.

Be kind to yourself in the process of hustling in Hollywood. You are going through a significant transformation as a human and a creative.

And so are many of the people around you, so be kind to them, too.

Go get 'em, tiger. Cheering you on!

Chapter Ten: Questions For Reflection

1) How are you winning life in LA? What is working really well for you that YOU have control over?

2) Do you have a community of healthy humans around you? If not, what's one step you can take this week to create that?

3) What can you pause right now to celebrate or be grateful for that is shaping your growth as a human?

4) What do you want someone to tell you right now that would fill you up with love and encouragement for your journey as a creative in LA? Write it down. Now read it back to yourself. You've got this.

Resources

While there are a lot of scams in Hollywood and people who will happily take your money for things like headshots, classes and workshops that will NOT get you to the professional level you want to be at, there are also some solid humans who are dedicated to providing knowledge and services to creatives in this city.

Like me. You might meet me on a darkened set some day or be trapped in a car as my rideshare driver, and I will be delighted to chat with you. Or, if you want a more surefire way to connect with me, contact me on Instagram (@melissacaddell) or email me: melissa.caddell@gmail.com

When I'm not looking for the good coffee at crafty, I am an Executive Coach and I will fiercely advocate for you and the vision you want for your life. I will help you get unstuck, get clear and get moving. Let's find that joy, shall we?

If a session with me would help you build a life you love or help you in your Hollywood hustle, I am happy to offer you a complimentary coaching session to get clear on what your vision is. Just reach out to me via the ways mentioned above and let's get you moving. I guarantee that something will happen.

As for other resources, I am listing a few places I have scoped out or know personally to be trustworthy. Use at your own discretion. Ask around, trust your instincts, and stay curious. If you find yourself avoiding/ procrastinating around connecting with something that you know will likely propel you forward, ask yourself why. Or message me and I'll ask you. :)

This is not an exhaustive list, but a place to start:

- Zak Barnett Studios - holistic actor training, lots of his students work!
- Margie Haber - lots of her students work, too!
- David Gray Studios - working actors, galore!
- Scott Sedita - the go-to guy for comedy training!
- John D'Aquino - have heard great things about him.
- Deadline Junkies LA - excellent screenwriting group
- Scriptnotes - super useful screenwriting podcast and website
- Backstage.com - really good knowledge base
- Heidi Dean - social media for actors, some good free resources
- Jenn Boyce / The Hollywood Prep - actor career coaching and info-lots of experience!
- Shading the Limelight - mental health services for creatives
- HappyActors.com - some good free resources
- TheCommercialClass.com - two of the top commercial casting directors have a workshop!
- creativepathsLA.com & melissacaddell.com - for

additional resources on how to have a thriving life and my signature program for creatives.

Come say hello on social media! @creativepathsLA and @melissacaddell

ACKNOWLEDGEMENTS

I am incredibly grateful for the support and wisdom of the people who helped me bring this book into existence. To the casting directors, producers, writers, directors, actors and crew who have generously shared their stories with me - thank you. Here's to you!

To Jenn Boyce (agent) and Nelson Paradez (manager) who first scouted Cameron at age 7 out of The Hollywood Showcase in Denver and started our family down this incredible path. What an adventure! Thank you.

Special shout-out to Su Coffey for her guidance and support through her showcase and in the years that followed as our family found our footing from Denver to LA!

The Savage Agency has been an incredible place for the girls to grow up in the industry. Stella Alex and Mark Smith have been some of the girls' biggest fans. And, wow, did we win the agent lottery with them! Not only for their industry connections and deep integrity, but because they are delightful humans. I am so grateful for the opportunities they have opened up for the girls as well as their fierce love and care for our family. Extra thanks to

Stella for sharing her incredible wisdom on the chapter on agents and managers.

Ever grateful to Nelson and his team at The ESI Network (mangers), including especially Garrett Lindsey, for their incredible vision of this business and teaching us that it is show BUSINESS. So glad to have them in our corner and all the work they do to guide the girls' careers. We are the grateful recipients of their wisdom, advocacy and expertise.

Thank you to Lauren Schmitke for her red pen prowess and keen eye! Her work to edit and clarify what I was trying to say has made this book more readable and resourceful.

And to Heather Rose Chase--lover of Los Angeles, writer and editor extraordinaire, cheerleader of creatives and taco aficionado--your many passes through this work were a true labor of love. Your questions and comments made it so much better. Just like you make me better. Los Angeles, creatives and tacos are lucky to have you as their #1 fan! And me. I'm super lucky to have you as my friend.

(Any errors are mine alone and are the result of being human and/or a coffee deficit.)

ABOUT THE AUTHOR

Melissa Caddell

Melissa Caddell is an award-winning author, an executive coach with the elite global firm Novus Global, and mom to three professional actors/creatives working in Hollywood. For 15 years she has accompanied her kids on set, mastering how to get good coffee at crafty while chatting with celebrities, writers, and other movers and shakers in Hollywood. In addition to discovering the best parking at casting studios in LA, she has asked lots of questions about why someone 'makes it' in Hollywood. Turns out, aside from parking info, working professional creatives in Hollywood are happy to share their wisdom. Melissa lives in Los Angeles with her husband, Casey, assorted daughters, and their pandemic shelter dog, Sokka.

Connect with her on social media, @melissacaddell and at: melissacaddell.com

(Author photo by Coco Lueng)

www.ingramcontent.com/pod-product-compliance
Lightning Source LLC
Chambersburg PA
CBHW021138020426
42331CB00005B/825